FORENSIC PSYCHOLOGY OF TERRORISM AND HOSTAGE-TAKING

CONNOR WHITELEY

DEDICATION

Thank you to all my readers without you I couldn't do what I love.

INTRODUCTION

Of all the extreme examples of criminal behaviour, like psychopaths, serial killers and more, there is one crime that creates so much interest and fascination that hundreds of myths and misconceptions get created to help people understand this most horrific example of criminal behaviour.

That is terrorism and hostage-taking.

Terrorism evokes, rightly, a lot of fear in people but a lot of interest and fascination as well. Since all of us are curious about what makes someone into a terrorist? Is it a combination of mental health or personality or social psychological factors?

This is what this book aims to investigate as we look into the forensic psychology research on terrorism. In this book, you'll learn about:

- What are the consequences of terrorism and why is it important to investigate?
- What makes a terrorist?

- How do people develop ideologies and mental processes supporting terror attacks?
- How do terror groups fall?
- And more.

If you want an engaging, easy-to-understand guide to terrorism and hostage-taking then you will love this book.

In addition, this book is for psychology students and professionals that want to understand the research on terrorism, including its limitations and the problem with terrorism research. All of this is explained in a fun, conversational tone that makes the material interesting and engaging.

Who Am I?

Personally, I always love to know who the author is of the nonfiction I read so I know the information is coming from a good source. In case you're like me, I'm Connor Whiteley, the internationally bestselling author of over 40 psychology books.

In addition, I am the host of *The Psychology World Podcast,* a weekly show exploring a new psychology topic each week and delivering the latest psychology news. Available on all major podcast apps and YouTube.

Finally, I am a psychology graduate studying a Clinical Psychology Masters at the University of Kent, England.

So now we know more about each other, let's dive into the great topic of terrorism and hostage-taking.

INTRODUCTION TO TERRORISM AND CONSEQUENCES OF TERRORISM

Before we explore a lot of great topics like what makes someone into a terrorist, what makes a suicide bomber and then we explore hostage situations, we need to understand why this is important at a larger scale first of all.

Therefore, terrorism is becoming of growing importance to governments over the past few decades because the public care about it and governments want to keep the public safe. For example, the UK's homeland security spend has increased from £1 billion in 2004 to £3 billion in 2009 (Mythen and Walklate, 2005) and it is estimated to be £3.5 billion in 2010/2011 (Secret Service, 2007). Therefore, as you can see governments are spending more and more on terrorism each year.

However, this is a little odd to some extent because terrorism actually doesn't kill that many people in the grand scheme of things.

Now please bear with me because I promise you there is a point here.

Since if we look at the United States of America, terrorism has killed at least 3,000 people in the decade of about 2005 to 2015, and the US spends about $0.5 billion on each death. Whereas stroke is the US's third largest killer and only $2,000 per death is spent (Sinn, 2017). You would have assumed that you would want to spend more on the larger killer, again there is a point explaining all of this later on.

Also, terrorism is low cost for the terrorist too because it only costs $150 to buy the materials needed for a suicide bomb large enough to kill 12 people on average (Lomborg, 2008).

What Are The Waves of Modern Terrorism?

When I first came across this research I was rather amazed because I do enjoy history and the history of terrorism and how it's evolved is certainly interesting and it helps to give the research we're going to be looking at a bit of a historical perspective to show how far terrorism has sadly come.

As a result, authors like Rapport (2004) and Post, McGinnis and Moody (2014) suggest there are 4 waves of modern terrorism. The first stage of modern terrorism started in 1880 with Anarchists in Russia spreading globally, and these anarchists used modern methods of communication effectively.

Secondly, the modern terrorism movement changed into the nationalist-anti-colonist movement between World War 1 and 2 where people sought to fulfil the mission of securing their nation's freedom from Imperial Masters.

Thirdly, modern terrorism morphed again into a social revolutionary wave that generally opposed the parent generation's ideals and this movement began in the 1960s. This sort of movement was frequently used in opposition against the Vietnam War. Like the weather man in USA or the shining path in Peru.

Fourthly, and this is a little more important for the current socio-political climate because we are sort of coming out of the end of this wave but a lot of the major terror events in the lives of you readers will be in this wave, modern terrorism changed in the 1980s to centre itself around religion. And this happened to a whole range of religions and this certainly wasn't just Islam. Then the use of social media highlights and supports the importance of communication that characterised modern terrorism according to Rapport.

Also, what's important to note about this fourth wave is that real fundamentalists employ mass destruction (Hudson, 1999) and this is something that seriously sets the fourth wave apart from previous waves of terrorism.

Since before this, terror groups had very different attitudes. For instance, before the fourth wave, terror groups like the IRA used to give specific warnings about their targets, now suicide is a weapon and tens can be killed instantly without warning.

Finally, in the past few years and a bit a new

wave has been added by Post et al. (2014) and this is the Lone-Wolf wave. Which I find a little scary to be honest because before it was entire groups wanting to commit terror groups but now Lone-wolves can commit terror attacks unlike before. They can find blueprints online for 3D printing guns and bomb parts. They can go down the shop can find everything you need for a fertilizer bomb (okay you could always do that option), but you don't need to be an organised group anymore to commit a terrorist attack.

That was a cheery paragraph. Sorry, that is the darkest I personally go in this book.

However, as you can see in this section of the chapter, whenever there is novel advancement in technology, like the advent of social media or mobile phones or other forms of communication, the wave of terrorism morphs into a new and different form.

The Research Problem Of Terrorism

Something you might notice fairly quickly in this book is that in the later chapters we will focus a little more on research studies, and we'll all notice that there is a massive, massive research problem in the terrorism field. This book tries to include some of the "best" studies but to be honest, even that is pushing it.

Due to there has been a lot of research into terrorism done over the past 40 years but the problem is that the vast majority of this research lacks empirical rigour (Borum, 2004) so this means the findings and the conclusions are hardly convincing.

Then again, something else I mention through the rest of the book is I suppose we need to have empathy to some extent. Since research terrorism is not easy, not only from a legal perspective but also from a participant recruitment viewpoint. As well as many of the most basic research methodologies cannot be used in terrorism research for the same reasons. For instance, I would rather like to know how would you use a semi-structured interview design. It's basic but it still gives us problems because terrorists are very unlikely to sit down with you and tell you everything you want to know. I would also like to know where are you going to find enough terrorists that are willing to talk to give your study some power, and finally I would like to know how researchers would overcome the classic forensic psychology problem of us typically only having access to prisoners. Also known as terrorists that got caught. This automatically skews our research because we have no idea about the behaviour of terrorists that haven't been caught.

All classic problems in forensic psychology research but the field of terrorism amplifies them.

As a result, this has led the vast majority of publications on terrorism to be only speculative or full of conjecture. Again this is not science.

Overall, terrorism research is avoided by mainstream psychology because of all these problems, and instead this research area survives in the cracks and crevices between disciplines like politics, sociology and psychology (Silker, 2004).

What Is The Nature Of Terrorism And How Do Terrorists Attack?

Another problem with terrorism research is the definition of what is terrorism? Logically speaking and a common sense definition is something along the lines of, a group of people who plan and carry out acts of violence with a political motive.

However, even though this is a fairly basic definition, it is far from perfect. Since this definition makes it difficult to differentiate terrorism from other forms of violence. For example, the sort of violence that can erupt at a political rally. That is violence with a political motive, but I really wouldn't say it's terrorism.

Therefore, there are a lot of questions that make creating a definition of terrorism very difficult.

In addition, there are databases that collect information from substantial data sets concerning terrorist incidents. Like the International Terrorism: Attributes of Terrorist Events (ITATE). And I'm mentioning this because these databases as well as other advanced statistical methods (like non-metric multi-dimensional scaling) were used by Yokota, Fjytam, Watanabe and Wachi (2007) to identify patterns in terrorism.

These analyses allowed the researchers to code each terrorist incident with a number of different dimensions so they were able to find common links with various strengths to create clusters.

As a result, three attack strategies emerged. Firstly, there is the "threat" strategy where terror groups seek to intimidate people and society and the aim here isn't to cause casualties. Secondly, there is the "mean" strategy where the victims are used as a way of negotiating the goals of the terror group. Thirdly, there is the "violence" strategy where the groups of people or individuals are targeted to be injured or killed by the terror groups.

I was somewhat surprised to learn that the most common attack strategy isn't violence, it is actually "threat" because 87% of terrorist organisations had over 50% of their incidents in that one group. Consequently, we can see that terrorist organisations don't stick to one strategy and it can vary so the researchers suggested that this small amount of variation could be a result of the instability within these terrorist organisations.

What Are The Consequences Of Terrorism?

Now this section really helps to put the rest of the book into perspective because it shows dealing with and understanding terrorism is beyond critical. The reason for this is because in society there is a general idea that the general public are extremely resilient against terrorism and it is because of this resilience that terrorism has minimal effect on the general public.

This is a lie society creates for itself obviously.

I say this because there's a lot of research showing that terrorism has profound effects on the general public. For example, DiMaggio and Galea (2006) show us results from a meta-analysis on the aftermath of terrorist incidents like 9/11 and the 2005 London Tube and bus bombings. Their results show that the rate of Post-Traumatic Stress Disorder for people were directly affected by the terrorism was between 12% to 16%. This shows us that being directly affected by a terrorist incident leads to the development of mental health conditions.

Another example can be seen in Gabriel et al. (2007) but for historical context, on the 11th March 2004 in Spain bombs exploded on 4 early commuter trains resulting in 400 people being taken to hospital and 200 people died, so Gabriel et al. (2007) wanted to study the aftermath on 3 different groups. The people injured in the blast, the people in the neighbourhood of the victims but didn't know them, and the final group was the police officers involved in the rescue.

The researchers interviewed members of each group on a one-on-one basis within 3 months and then the researchers used standard diagnostic instruments like the mini-international neuropsychiatric interview and Davidson Trauma Scale to assess the mental health of participants.

Their results showed the injured group had the most evidence of current mental health conditions

11

with 58% of them meeting a criteria for diagnosis. Then 26% of the local area group had the criteria and then only 4% of the police officers did. The most common mental health condition was PTSD at 44%.

And what was really interesting about this data was the sheer amount of comorbidity because 53% of the injured group showed comorbidity compared to 22% of the local area group.

Therefore, compared to the last study we looked at, this gives us clearer results on the impact of direct victimisation on victims but also secondary victimisation too. Since if secondary victimisation wasn't an outcome of terrorism then the local group should have seen results like the police officers, but it is clear the people in the neighbourhoods of the victims were profoundly affected by the terrorist attack.

Additionally, DiMaggio, Galea and Richardson (2007) found that 9/11 caused an increase of mental health admissions to hospitals and the closer you were to the attack, the likelihood of you developing a mental health condition increased.

As well as Jhangiani (2010) reviewed 18 studies into psychological consequences of the 9/11 attack and their results showed evidence of people experiencing poorer mental health after the New York and Washington D.C attacks. Although, the review did show that people's mental health returned to pre-attack levels quickly about 6 months after the attacks, or some studies suggested it was better soon after the attack.

The precise details of this improvement vary case to case but the negative mental health outcomes of terrorist attacks aren't permeant.

Also, the effects of a terrorist attack were worse if a person had a history of mental health conditions beforehand, if they knew someone involved like a victim, if they were physically very close to the attack but if they were outside the attack area they experienced a more minimal effect of the attack.

Overall, whilst positive responses to terror attacks were useful in the long-term in increasing helping behaviour and even increase life satisfaction, this chapter so far has still shown us the deadly and foul consequences that terrorist attacks have on society. Especially, when we consider that all of us can be considered victims of terrorist attacks directly or indirectly because of primary and secondary victimisation.

What Affects Our Response To Attacks?

Speaking of positive responses to terrorist attacks, let's see what impacts our responses. Ferguson and Kamble (2012) studied the responses of UK and Indian students to the Mukai terrorist attacks of 2008. These terrorist attacks involved a series of bombing with a minimum of 173 dead and lots more injured and these researchers decided to examine the effect of the Just World Beliefs (Lerner, 1980) on helping responses. And in case you're unfamiliar with

Just World Beliefs, the short answer is that if people believe in Just World Beliefs then they believe that you get what you deserve in life. For example, if you're a victim of a terrorist attack then you're getting your just desserts for some wrong you have previously done.

The reason why these researchers choose to study Just World Beliefs is because when dreadful events happen these aren't easily reconciled with these Just World Beliefs, because at first people with Just World Beliefs want to help others but they can also blame victims for their poor character or responsibilities.

Therefore, Ferguson and Kamble boiled it down to people believing we get what we deserve and get what's coming to us.

However, the results surprised the researchers a lot because the participants completed the Global Beliefs in Just World Scale (Lipkus, 1991) and (remember this was a terrorist attack against India) and the results showed Indian students had more Just World beliefs than UK students. Now this could be down to cultural differences and Indian students had higher levels of terrorism-related distress, more desire for revenge and higher levels of terrorism denial. Regardless of the Just World Belief, those higher in Just World Beliefs tended to have higher levels of a desire for revenge and terrorism denial.

The researchers concluded that these findings suggest this shows multiple strategies are used to maintain belief in a Just World. Which makes sense when we consider that Just World Beliefs can be used to improve someone's self-esteem and other psychological benefits because it helps them to feel that the world isn't chaotic and it's a safe place.

Overall, at the end of this chapter, we can conclude that the public's response to terrorist attacks are complex judging from the available research, and systemic research into terrorism is difficult because it is difficult to plan and has to be done quickly. Also, this makes it hard to be systematic and theoretical in orientation compared to being pragmatic about the aims of study.

In addition, if we go back to what I say at the very beginning of the chapter, there is a reason why governments spend so much money on anti-terrorism because whilst the research generally accepts that terrorists seek to scare the public to put pressure on governments to comply with them, in reality governments don't seek to reduce this fear but to maintain it at a high level (Braithwaite, 2013). Since Braithwaite suggests this could be to avoid the government being blamed for saying the public are safe when they're not. But this could be because this level of fear makes the public alert so they report things that suggest an attack is coming.

Personally, I was rather shocked when I first read that but it makes sense and in the grand scheme f things, I would much rather have a base level of fear and be alert for terrorist activity then think the world was extremely safe, only to be the victim of a terror attack.

So after this great introduction to terrorism, are there any personality or mental health factors that could make someone into a terrorist?

IS THERE A TERRORIST PERSONALITY OR MENTAL HEALTH CONDITION? AND SUICIDE BOMBERS

Now I absolutely have to admit I flat out cringe whenever I see academics or psychology students talking about a "terrorist or criminal personality" or whether a mental health condition has led to a particular behaviour. I tend to cringe because as you'll find out about in this chapter, it is extremely, extremely unlikely that a personality trait or a mental health condition will lead someone to become a terrorist or a criminal.

I think the only real reason why these debates happen in the first place is because these debate pop up in mainstream culture from the media, politicians and different conversations between friends and family. Then academics want to test out the idea, and to be honest, I might be being a little critical here but we do need to rule out these personality and mental health factors so it is good that this research has been conducted.

Although, because my background is in clinical psychology, I want to say upfront here that I will not be using the terms psychopathology or mental disorder or mental illness in this book unless a paper has specifically used it and I want to reuse it for a reason. This is because modern clinical psychology understands how blaming, judgmental and unhelpful these terms are. Since mental health conditions, like depression and anxiety, are a part of a person and they cannot be cured. They don't mean anything is wrong with a person. And instead, it is our job as current or future clinical psychologists to help people improve their coping mechanisms so they can live full lives.

Anyway, that's me done on my soapbox.

Therefore, in this chapter, we'll be exploring some of this research before we move onto talking about suicide bombers.

Is There A Terrorist Personality?

One of the main reasons in academia why this personality strain of research has popped up is because extremists are very hard to conceptualise. Since are they all mad (I hate that term)? Are they all strong? Are they all suicide prone?

On the whole, it is very tempting to label terrorist actions as insane and the result of some personality factor or mental health condition. Yet this is very unhelpful for the clinical populations that actually have mental health conditions as this perpetuates and creates stigma that shouldn't be there in the first place.

Moreover, it is dangerous to label certain actions as one thing when the truth is a lot, lot more complex than that given label. For example, the media feeds laypeople the idea that all suicide bombers are religious zealots but this isn't true in the slightest. Since the Tami tigers of Sri Lanka are political suicide bombers with operations all over the world.

Another false assumption is that it is the male sex that exclusively performs suicide bombings, but there are a surprising amount of women that partake in these terrorism acts. For example, the Tami Tigers of Sri Lanka and Kurdistan Workers party use women bombers as much as men (Ergil, 2001).

Consequently, it isn't empirically correct at all to say that suicide bombers are simply religious extremists.

Overall, there is remarkable consensus that that there is no terrorist personality (Silk, 2004) and stressing and having conversations about there being no mental abnormality is also important when dealing with terrorists.

One academic that tries to explain this is Borum (2004, 2014) because this researcher summarised the literature saying that terrorism is poorly explained by psychopathology. And of course, some terrorism will be explained by mental health conditions, but far from all of it is.

What About A Terrorist Profile?

As someone who wrote a bestselling *Criminal Profiling* book that explores the truth about how horrifically bad criminal profiling is, this makes me laugh because any sort of "profiles" are just setting up researchers to fail. Because guess what? Humans are all different so they can't be accurately profiled.

Anyway, this is a real shocker but there are no useful constructed profiles of terrorists. Since Maghan (1998) explained that terrorists cover all types of people from the self-doubting wreck to those haunted by their personal demons, but madness or mental disorders have no role to play as an explanatory concept for why someone becomes a terrorist.

This is supported by Ruby (2002) as well who commented terrorists are rational, lucid people, with Silke (1998) supporting this finding too. As well as Ariel Merari at the university of Tel Avia studied 32 suicide bombers and she found no evidence of suicidality or social dysfunction which would account for their actions.

Again, even more evidence that terrorism isn't caused by mental health conditions.

One of the reasons for these findings is because terror groups take advantage of new recruits having religious fanaticism and nationalism instead of mental health conditions, but even this nationalism and fanaticism fails to account for why some people and not others become suicide bombers.

As a result, Merari and other researchers argue that terrorists are normal people who are a cross-section of society with there being no significant evidence of mental health conditions amongst them.

What About Terrorism And Psychopathy?

It's still understandable though why people think there is a link between mental health and terrorism, because the vast majority of terrorist acts are atrocities and difficult for people to understand. For example, the humiliation of hostages and the slow videotaped beheadings of them led to questions of psychopathy. Another reason why this is understandable is because we know that psychopaths commit some horrific and strange murders.

Leading some researchers to review this assumption and one such researcher was Borum (2004) who found that psychopaths aren't good fits for any organisation (in slight contradiction to other studies) because whilst selflessness and dedication might be required of terrorists, these two major characteristics are extremely, extremely different to the characteristics showed by psychopaths.

Therefore, I think after all these studies, all these different aspects of mental health and personality factors, we can confirm that someone doesn't become a terrorist because of a mental health condition or personality factors. Or at least the vast, vast majority of them do not.

If It Isn't Caused By Mental Health Conditions Or Personality Factors Why Do People Become

Terrorists?

Whilst we talk about this again in the next chapter, we can draw on social psychology research to explain this because the subdiscipline shows how good people can do bad things as part of normal social processes. I think everyone reading this book is familiar with good old Milgram and his 1974 study where he showed that obedience is a powerful force and can make university students electrocute someone pass the point of death. Then a lot of other research that looked into why different things happened in World War two proves the same point.

In addition, one of my favourite little references I've discovered in the course of my research for this book was made by Taylor and Quayle (1994) because they asked the very simple question of we don't expect all university students to be the same or even similar, so why do we expect terrorists to be the same?

It's a good point and this is why I flat out hate "profiling" and any sort of research that investigates the profiles of certain people. These researchers are always setting themselves up for failure.

As a result, Borum (2014) suggested the study of terrorism might progress faster if the field adopts more complex models of how people's psychology involving normal mental states and processes might explain why a person might become involves in terrorist activity.

Here Borum acknowledges that there is contextual and environmental factors going on here because terrorism is more common in some settings compared to others, and a person's worldview (which is different to personality) is important in them becoming a terrorist too. For example, the 4 Borum mentioned is Authoritarianism, dogmatism, fundamentalism and apocalypticism.

Now authoritarianism is important in terrorism research (and basically everything social psychology looks at) because this is a learnt attitude about being hostile and aggressive towards outgroups and submissiveness towards authority figures as well as being conservative. This is useful to terrorism because it means the person is more likely to take part in aggressive and hostile acts towards outgroups whilst being submissive and following orders from the leadership.

Similar to authoritarianism, dogmatism needs to be looked at here because a dogmatic person manifests a very closed set of strongly held beliefs and disbeliefs that are resistant to change. For example, any beliefs about how evil outgroups are and why they all need to be cleansed in fire. As well as dogmatic people need authority as absolute and are generally intolerant of most other people.

Whereas fundamentalist thinking involves a person having absolutist religious thinking about right and wrong and how people are categorised morally. In other words, whatever their religion says about a person that is it and they aren't going to change their minds about it. also, paranoia is a characteristic of fundamentalists as well as they rage against those who they believe have humiliated them. In terms of leadership this group of people are led by a charismatic leader who has intense conviction.

Then finally, apocalypticism is an aspect of fundamentalism and involves the belief of a future catastrophic event with only a few people having been warned of the event so they can be the most prepared for it and survive.

In addition, Borum suggests there is more to a person becoming involved in terrorism than personality and mental health factors. For example, the number of psychological vulnerabilities and number of propensities they have for terrorist activity. This is similar to how people get involved in cults as I talk about in my book, *Cult Psychology*.

As a result, terror groups can take advantage of these psychological vulnerabilities and make them have a role in "shaping" a person's thoughts and actions that can lead to an increased risk of getting involved with terrorism.

These psychological vulnerabilities can include, a person's need to belong, their need for meaning and identity as well as a person's perception of injustice and humiliation. All these are risk factors for terrorism because belonging to a terror group fulfils a lot of these needs for different people. Such as a terror group could provide someone with a chance to rectify the perceived injustice and humiliation, it gives them a family and something to belong to and it could give them a sense of meaning and purpose in their lives that helps to make up their identity.

Therefore, it isn't hard to see how an injustice or humiliation, like living under an occupying army, could push someone towards terrorism.

Also, it's important to consider how a person's motivational, attributional, attitudinal and volitional propensities of various types could also play a role in whether or not they become involved in terrorism. For example, the hostile attribution bias is the tendency to see hostility in what others say or do so it isn't hard to see how this links to terrorism. As people inclined towards terrorism might see an outgroup as speaking in a threatening way towards them in a preparation of an attack so terrorism might be a way for the person to strike first or something like that.

Overall, the entire point of this chapter so far has been to show that the psychology of terrorism research doesn't need to focus on mental health conditions as an explanation and instead this research area can be directed towards more ordinary psychological processes.

Suicidal Characteristics And Suicide Terrorism

I preluded to and briefly spoke about suicide bombers earlier in the chapter but now we need to focus on them a little more. Since suicide bombers are relatively rare in terrorism but they account for a high proportion of terrorism-related deaths.

And this is such an important thing to say that I have to say it upfront. We CANNOT regard suicide bombers as suicidal people because this flat out isn't how suicide bombers think, act or feel. Since Silke (2003) found that suicide bombers don't share the characteristics and motivations of typical people who want to commit suicide. As well as if you want to learn more about the psychology behind suicide, please check out *Suicide Psychology* for more information.

In addition, suicide bombers are actually psychologically stable people and they have very ordinary personalities when judged within their own culture. Meaning yet again, terrorists aren't mad or insane and terrorism cannot be explained by personality factors.

Also, the families of suicide bombers regard their relative's actions as positive and heroic. This and more is supported by Townsend (2007)'s views on the question of if suicide bombers are suicidal. Due to this is technically difficult to answer because the strategy was to assess the similarities and differences between what we know from suicide research as a whole and what we know from research on potential suicide bombers.

However, that is the first reason why this is a technically difficult question because we cannot conduct research on people who have successfully (I seriously hate that word) committed suicide and suicide bombers, because they are dead. Therefore, we can only conduct research on potential suicide bombers because these people never actually carried out the attack, thankfully.

Nonetheless, the research has shown that there is little correlation between suicidal people and suicide bombers and there are no typical range of motivations that link the two together.

In fact, mental health is a lot higher in the suicide bomber group because suicide bombers tend to have feelings of martyrdom and other positive feelings and in the service of Allah. As well as this type of Martyrdom is known as Istishahad (Abdel-Khalek, 2004).

This is important to bear in mind because suicide is not acceptable at all in Islam (and that alone has extremely damaging mental health implications for everyone in society but that is way beyond the scope of this book, but I talk more about that *Suicide Psychology*).

Furthermore, another interesting mismatch between suicide research and suicide bomber research is that there is some research that shows being religious is a protective factor against suicide (Nonemaker, McNelly and Blum, 2003). This further explains why suicide bombers aren't suicidal.

Also, whilst suicidal people might be motivated by their desire to end their pain and stop being a burden on the world (even though they are more loved than they'll ever know and life gets better), suicide bombers are motivated by vengeance. As well as suicidal people rarely feel vengeance and even then they don't want to harm others before their suicide.

However, there is at least one study that shows this isn't always the case because Merari, Diamont, Bibi, Broshi and Zakin (2010) found that 53% of suicide bombers had depressive and suicidal symptoms compared to only 21% of suicide bombing organisers and 8% of non-suicide bomber insurgents. Also, exclusive to suicide bombers was 40% showed suicidal tendencies that were not associated in their desire for martyrdom.

These are some interesting findings because they show that a small majority of suicide bombers could have their actions explained away by mental health conditions. But what about the remaining 47%, that is a massive amount of suicide bombings that aren't explained by mental health.

In response to that study, these results were strongly criticised by Bryon and Araj (2012) who suggested that these differences were not statistically significant and the judgement of the symptoms could have been wishful thinking on the part of researchers.

To support their argument, Bryon and Araj (2012) used evidence from a study of the Palestinian family and close friends of suicide bombers. And this study tell very different stories to Merari et al.'s because 76% of the suicide bombers showed no signs of depression or of personal crisis as far as the close friends or family knew.

As well as in the other 24%, the depression could have been down to political or social factors. And whatever the answer, depression rates for Palestinians living in Gaza or the West Bank was much the same.

The Need For Risk Assessments

To finish up this chapter, we need to talk about risk assessments for terrorists because how we actually go about rehabilitating terrorists has become a very practical and important concern for governments in recent years.

And before I continue, please allow me to jump on my little soapbox again. Rehabilitation works, there is a lot of psychological research showing that offenders that have been rehabilitated are much less likely to reoffend. That means these rehabilitated offenders are much less likely to commit crimes, have to go through the criminal justice system which costs taxpayer money and they don't need to go to prison which costs a lot of taxpayer money. So I know I am probably talking to the choir here but please don't dismiss the amazing power of rehabilitating criminals just because your local politician says it shouldn't be done. Please, read the research and then make an informed decision.

Anyway, Horgan and Bradlock (2010) reviewed a number of de-radicalisation programmes, and the researchers found that with terrorists having a lack of mental health conditions and us assuming that terrorists are psychologically normal. This presents psychologists with a massive problem because to have prisoners released from prison, a risk assessment needs to be done. But how do you carry out a risk assessment and determine the risk to the general public against future terrorist activity if they're psychologically normal and have no mental health conditions. There is basically no "warning signs" to look out for.

In addition, it's worth noting here that normally risk assessments work brilliantly and they do their job. But we don't know at this point in time how well these risk assessment apply to terrorists because these risk assessments are based on other non-terrorist prisoners and psychiatric patients.

Terrorists have nothing in common with either group as we've discussed in this chapter.

Moreover, Dernevick, Beck and Grams, Hogue and McGuire (2009a) argued that psychologists and psychiatrists don't have the knowledge base to formulate risk assessments for terrorists, because the current approaches, like risk to the public and chance of reoffending, cannot be applied to terrorists. Mainly because terrorist violence is so different to "normal" interpersonal violence.

Also, Dernevick et al. (2009a) were particularly concerned about the value of psychometric tests as these tests were developed on very different groups of offenders to terrorists. As well as there are other problems in establishing this risk assessment methodology. For example, the researchers pointed out how different groups of terrorists come from different routes. This can be seen in the last chapter when we were talking about the 5 waves of terrorism, all of those people came from extremely different routes depending on the wave they belonged too. And even though to be honest there's likely to be hundreds of different routes within each other.

As a result, we cannot think of terrorists as reoffending criminals as showed by Sagiman (2004) who showed that members of the worldwide fundamentalist network that Al-Qaeda is a part of, have no criminal history besides a couple of very small minor offences. He found that these members had no mental health conditions according to the DSM-4 as well.

On the whole, this means that the lack of a criminal history cannot be used to predict reoffending in terrorists, because the current method would say once they're released they present a very low risk to the public because they have no criminal history.

We don't know if this "very low" risk is true or false or extremely false at this point in time.

Interestingly, Gudjonsson (2009) regarded Dernevick et al. (2009a) somewhat negatively. As they responded by saying that some motivations of the terrorism might have changed or been removed by the time the terrorist is released from prison due to the political and motivational changes that might occur. For example, there's no research done on this at the moment at the time of writing, but the West's withdrawal from Afghanistan might be an example of this. It might be possible that the West's withdrawal might mean some terrorists might leave the organisation as they might perceive that the goals of their terror group have been achieved.

I don't know but it is just a thought and a question that I hope future research addresses.

One of the few recommendations about risk assessment for terrorists has been looking into the possible terrorist support network that a person might be able to plug themselves back into to once they're released. The idea here being if a prisoner cannot get back in contact with their terrorist network then they might not reoffend. This isn't traditionally done in risk assessments but I think this is going to have to be done in terrorism cases.

Although, I have to admit there is still a problem with this approach because of the 5th wave of terrorism. With lone-wolf terrorism becoming the new thing, I doubt a person would need a terrorist network to reoffend and become a very active terrorist once again.

WHAT MAKES A TERRORIST?

If a terrorist isn't made by personality factors or mental health conditions, then how does a person become a terrorist? This is the focus of this chapter and something we'll be exploring in a lot of depth.

The general consensus is that it takes time to convert a vulnerable person into a terrorist (Luckabaugh et al., 1997) because this is a process and different terrorist recruits have different motivations. For example, a need to belong, the development of a satisfactory personal identity, social alienation and boredom leads to dissidence and protests on a small scale, then over time terrorism, as well as histories of child abuse, trauma, humiliation and social injustice are common in a terrorist's background as well.

Although, Borum (2004) doesn't feel like this is helpful in explaining terrorism, because these factors are vulnerabilities and they don't make someone a terrorist on their own. Also, Merari (2007) may be suggesting general vulnerability factors when he suspects susceptibility to indoctrination is key to understanding suicide bombers. Due to most of the suicide bombers Merari studied where young and unattached people which are perfect types for all sorts of violent organisations.

As a result, Merari believed suicide terrorism could be understood as consequences of a terrorist system, with people being recruited through interpersonal connections that then supported the recruit all the way through to becoming a suicide bomber.

This is important to learn about because highly committed members of an organisation will spend hours talking to recruits, promoting the idea of martyrdom as will of the God and they focus on the illustrious past of Islam. Then the recruits become enmeshed in the group contact that is designed to help the recruit prove their allegiance to the organisation. Afterwards this "formal contract" creates a final personal commitment before a suicide bomber attack.

In addition, Merari compared terror groups to suicide bomb production lines using empirical support from Palestinian suicide bombers.

The stages of these production lines according to Merari include indoctrination. This is where members of terror groups with high authority constantly indoctrinate potential bombers to maintain their motivation to engage in the terrorist act and to prevent them changing their mind.

For Palestinian indoctrination, the themes were nationalism. For instance, Israel's humiliation of the Palestinian state and religious guarantees, by saying things like the suicide bomber will go to paradise after committing this act. As well as getting the recruit to commit to the group is done too at this stage where any doubts about committing to the attack are dealt with and the motivation for the attack is increased to maximum levels, or "maxed out" to use more urban slang terms.

Then the last stage is personal commitment and this can take the form of video recordings were the terrorist describes their intent to do the suicide bombing. This is partly done for their family, but it is also done as a way of getting irreversible commitment. As well as the bomber prepares farewell letters for friends and family too for later giving.

Also, at this point in the production line, Merari points out these would-be bombers are called "Living-Martyr", and this whole approach is sympathetic with Horgan and Taylor (2001)'s view that terrorists don't actively choose to become terrorists.

Instead becoming a terrorist is a gradual process where a potential terrorist is socialised with the recruiters having the ultimate goal of making them preform a terrorist act.

Of course, this is a process and not an absolute. People can leave the process at any point and this is to be expected given the high turnover rate in terrorist group membership (Crenshaw, 1986).

Moreover, Taylor and Louis (2004) suggested young people find themselves wanting a hopeful future and they engage in meaningful behaviour that helps them get ahead and will be satisfied with their life. Also, these young people's objective circumstances include no opportunity for a good future or advancement, and whilst they might find some collective identity in religions, living in a poor state and community makes them feel marginalised and lost without a clear group.

So it's easy to think how terror acts are result of group processes with Taylor (2010) asking can terrorism truly be understood as a phenomenon of group behaviour. Since Taylor (2010) distinctives between getting involved in a terror group and actually carrying out attacks.

Since group processes could be important as a backdrop in terrorism when cultural, political and social factors have a role to play. But these group processes fail to explain the act or episode of terrorism itself.

Taylor suggests there are two main issues with the "terrorism as group processes" argument. There is a lack of a good definition of what is terrorism besides from what terrorists do, and there isn't a clear idea of what is meant by group processes in relation to terrorism. Since there are times when group processes seem to play no or little role in a terrorist attack. Lone-wolf attacks spring to mind here.

Another extreme example is the reclusive Theodore John Kaczynski who's terrorist campaign lasted for 17 years with 12 bombs and 3 deaths for his environmental agenda that he largely made-up alone without a group behind him.

What Are Life Story Studies?

I do enjoy qualitative research and I think given how hard terrorism is to research, qualitative research methodologies might be useful. Of course, you will still have a lot of the same problems as the rest of terrorism research as I wrote about in the first chapter but qualitive research can still be useful.

Especially as Borum (2004) argued that a terrorist's life experience includes common themes. He suggests that these common themes aren't sufficient causes of terrorism, but they might be helpful to researchers to identify people susceptibility to being influenced by terrorist groups.

In some ways this argument fits with the narrative studies being done with terrorists because they reveal other factors are needed to understand what turns someone into a terrorist and it helps to show that not all terrorists are made because of their similar circumstances. That notion doesn't really have research support anymore.

In addition, since 1992, terrorism has been a feature of "Israel's relationship with Palestine" and Soibelman (2004) subscribes to the group processes idea over individual's psychology like personality. Due to the researcher rejects the idea that suicide bombers are simply young religious fanatics and instead believes less extreme personality characteristics make up bombers. This was based on his research and interviews with 5 suicide bombers that were arrested before they could carry out the attack or the bombs failed to detonate (something that happens in another 40% of suicide bombings). The results of his interviews show there wasn't a single explanation for why they became terrorists and instead there was a mixture of factors that were responsible but even this mixture was different for different terrorists.

Yet it seemed that group solidarity and having a shared ideology were two overriding factors in becoming a terrorist because most of the interviewed suicide bombers had at least some shared ideology and solidarity.

Furthermore, political factors were given as reasons for becoming suicide bombers, as well as having bad or secondary experience of dealing with the Israeli defence force. Such as the Israelis shooting one of their friends or beating them.

And this is what I find interesting, most of the suicide bombers had been involved in protests or another form of assembly beforehand they were involved in terrorism. That means these people once wanted change through peaceful means and something changed to make them believe terrorism was the only option.

To explain this, Soibelman (2004) suggested as the situation escalates, a person's beliefs get more extreme. As well as given the nature of the sample, these suicide bombers were a part of the secular Fatah movement, so religion wasn't a factor in them becoming terrorists. And despite this terrorist group don't tend to have criminal histories, a few of them could have.

Another study that offers up a more detailed account of the range of factors impacting someone's chance of becoming a terrorist can be found in Sarangi and Alison's (2005) and their study of the left-wing Maoist terrorists in Nepal and India. This terror group believe the state is an instrument of the rich and needs to be violently overthrown.

The researchers interviewed 12 terrorists and 3 men and 3 women that were no longer involved with their average age being 26 years old and they generally lacked a formal education. These interviews were validated by checking court and police records.

In this study, rapport building was a priority and the researches achieved this by having the terrorists talk about their childhood and matters not directly tied to terrorist activities. Then the researchers suggested common rhetorical structures in the interview.

The results of the interviews showed that the terrorists had created a strong sense of "Us" (which included their Self-Image) and they saw themselves as a central character for themselves in their life story as brave, good, simple, logical and so on. Instead of the reality when the terrorist spoke about themselves, their family, friends and other people in their community being poor simple, naive, exploited, short on goods and water and cheated by others.

Also, the interviews showed interpersonal figures were important and included rhetoric about outgroups and others. For example, one rhetoric found was about their beliefs surrounding the government being characteristic of rich, powerful, villain, uncaring and inhuman.

Overall, this study found that terrorists believe themselves to be heroes and very good people that are fighting against an outgroup that is evil and foul and needs to be defeated. This sense of them being heroes helps them maintain their positive self-image and they see their friends and family and local communities as suffering at the hands of the outgroup. Hence, why the outgroup needs to suffer for this perceived injustice.

In conclusion, if these past two chapters have taught you anything, I think we have to conclude that there really is no single factor that causes someone to become a terrorist. It is a mixture of individual, group and political factors that interact together to help make people into a terrorist.

So now we understand how terrorists are made, how do terrorist ideologies and mental processes supporting these extreme ideologies develop?

FORENSIC PSYCHOLOGY OF TERRORISM AND HOSTAGE-TAKING

TERRORIST IDEAOLOGIES AND COGNITION

At this point in the book, we've looked at an introduction to terrorism, any personality or mental health factors that could cause someone to become a terrorist and all of these explanations have basically failed to explain how a terrorist ideology and cognition develops. Therefore, let's zero in on this research area and ask ourselves this pressing question.

Since I think we can all understand that it must take a very specific set of cognitive factors for someone to develop an ideology and set of mental processes that support bombings, mass terror events and other acts of terrorism, like hostage-taking.

As a result, this area of research focuses on the ideological and cognitive changes that are common to help us understand the terrorist journey. Therefore, Borum (2004) proposes that in order to understand terrorism, it is critical to understand that terrorist ideologies are often favourable towards and justify a particular pattern. As well as these ideologies involve an erosion of normal human inhibitions against killing because of the influence of environmental and social changes in the perception of the situation.

This is a logical argument because the vast majority of us have done social psychology before and we understand the importance of people maintaining a positive self-image, so it makes sense that a person would have to develop cognitive processes justifying and supporting their actions. Otherwise, they would feel bad about themselves and no one wants that for self-image and mental health reasons.

In addition, Brown (2004) argued there are 3 conditions that result in a person developing an ideology supporting terrorism. These conditions are the ideology must be characteristic by rigid orthodoxies that don't allow these beliefs to be challenged or questioned in any way. Also, the terrorist ideology must involve beliefs that both justify and guide the terrorist acts.

This is similar to what we saw earlier in the book about True Believers, suicide bombers and more. They truly believe what they're doing is right and when their leadership asks them to act, they don't question their actions regardless of whoever it kills.

Furthermore, building upon the point I made earlier about how terrorist maintain a positive self-image, Bandura (1990) refers to an techniques of moral disengagement. This is important because this disengagement from morality allows terrorists to insulate themselves from the psychological consequences of their actions.

Some of these moral disengagement strategies include dehumanising the victim and coming up with various moral justifications. For example, their act of terrorism is them fighting some evil or grand injustice. As well as other strategies include, minimizing the suffering of their victims and displacement of responsibility by shifting it from themselves to their leaders or others in group. Therefore, this allows the terrorists to disown their agency in the act.

Finally, Beck (2002) demonstrated how terrorists exhibit thinking that shows cognitive distortions that are similar to the distortions found in non-terrorists that carry out violent acts. For instance, terrorists overgeneralise the enemy's failings to encompass whole populations instead of who's really at fault, their perceptions are very white and black with no grey areas as well as terrorists form tunnel vision by focusing on deconstruction of targets.

On the whole, by the end of this chapter, we can see that there are a number of different cognitive changes that develop within a person that allows them to develop a terrorist ideology and cognition. These cognitive changes include using moral disengagement strategies, cognitive distortions and developing rigid orthodoxies that result in their actions being unquestioned.

As heartbreaking as this all is because of the horrific outcomes terrorism can cause, I think this is really interesting to look at because it allows us to understand that social and environmental causes do have a massive impact on a person's behaviour. But also, if we understand how these cognitive changes happen in the first place then we can hopefully start to apply this research in ways that allow us to target these cognitions in deradicalisation programmes.

So now we understand the cognition of a terrorist, we have to ask ourselves the very interesting question of, how do terrorists plan terror attacks?

HOW DO TERRORISTS PLAN TERROR ATTACKS?

Now as a mystery writer, this topic got me very excited to learn about because there are times when I need to know how terrorists might react and plan out an attack. As well as I generally think that everyone is interested in this topic because it can't be easy planning a terror attack when we consider security, finding a target and getting the resources together in order to carry out the attack.

Therefore, when I found out there was "research" on this topic I was rather excited.

However, yet again, we need to accept that this is a very difficult area to research because it's hard to get viable data, because what terrorist would want to reveal how they planned an attack?

Not many.

As a result, researchers have settled for a much less empirical approach to the topic of planning terror attacks. It is even so bad that there are entire academically published articles that contain no data. Instead they are simply speculative, conjecture or entirely theoretical in nature.

Personally, I don't really blame the researchers because they are trying to research the impossible and this must be difficult. Yet psychology is a science so they should at least attempt to be empirical about it and collect empirically validate data to support and draw conclusions from.

Anyway, as you can tell, there is a desperate need for empirical data on the topic.

Thankfully, there's an approach to research by Romyn and Kebbell (2013) that helps us to fill in this gap to some extent. Since these researchers stimulated the planning of a terrorist attack using non-terrorists. For their study, they had "Red Team" Australians in 2 groups with no anti-terrorism training and then another single group with anti-terrorism training.

Then there was Blue Team who was meant to anticipate how the Red Team would attack as well as this group was made up of people with anti-terrorism training like police officers.

The results of the study showed that all the groups ranked the steps involved in planning an attack as the same regardless of their training, but there were differences in how important each step was. For example, the step of "getting weapons" and "identifying targets" were seen as the most important. Also, there was a lot of consistency in targets chosen by the different groups.

As a result of the most popular targets were:

- Underground railway station
- Football cup final
- Military march
- Airport
- Religious gathering
- Electrical substations
- Military base

In addition, there were a lot of similarities in the ordering of targets between the Red and Blue teams with the main reason for the targets being chosen as the expectation of higher causalities and security. As well as the stages involved in the attack. For example:

- Selection of targets
- Get information from internet
- Select location of attack
- In-person recon of location
- Acquire necessary weapons
- Test the weapons

Personally, I think this is rather useful and interesting because it shows us how normal non-terrorists might go about researching and planning a terror attack. And I suppose the mystery writer in me gets interested in the possible storylines that can come off this study. For example, what would happen if some participants who took part in this research then wanted to make their attack real? That would be a lot of fun to write up actually.

However, I have to admit that this research has very limited usefulness in reality, because it is so artificial. These aren't even terrorists for starters so they would lack the drive, the motivation and to be honest, probably the resources to even pull this off. Then again, that might not be much of a valid criticism because of the new wave of lone wolf terrorists.

As a result, future research would dramatically need to improve the methodology and hopefully future research would include interviews with retired or captured terrorists.

So now we understand how terrorists plan terror attacks, what happens when terrorist organisations collapse?

HOW DO TERRORIST ORGANISATIONS END?

I think the vast majority of the content in this book are topics that we think about once in a while. For example, what do all terrorists have a mental health condition, how do terrorists plan attacks and later on, why do people take hostages? Yet even I have to admit that no one really thinks about terrorist organisations ending, until we're asked too.

I suppose in a way one of the only major terrorist organisations that I know about ending is Islamic State and then now I think about it, I know the Ireland Republican Army ended in the 70s. Yet both of those organisations have morphed and changed and returned as something else, just nothing as powerful as they once were.

Therefore, we need to learn upfront that terrorist organisations do end and this is a very poorly understood area of research. Partly this is because it's relatively new and it's only started to receive research interest recently, but also because you really have to be watching terrorist organisations to realise when they've started, when was their peak year and when they've ended.

One research study looking at this topic is Reinares (2011) who interviewed former members of Euskadi Ta Askatasuma (ETA) who had left the organisation before it closed in the 2000s. The researchers found that the key to the organisation's fall was the death of Spanish Dictator Franco in 1975 as Spain became a democracy and there was political decentralisation.

For the ETA's members these political and social changes were enough. And the Basques people were also changing their attitudes towards separatism and violence. In other words, members believed the terror group had achieved its aims so there was no longer any point in being active members. Whereas other people left for reasons that can only be described as personal.

As well as it's worth noting that the members who left didn't become more militant or deracialised, and some former members still strongly believed in the doctrines of violence they agreed to when they joined. Therefore, we could judge that sometimes terrorists leave organisations not because they don't belief in the "mission" anymore or because they're too militant or disillusioned with the organisation, they could leave for personal or other reasons.

In addition, other former members were expelled by the ETA leadership and there were some findings on the circumstances of the members abandoning membership which was useful as it shed some light on the topic.

Due to some people left the ETA when they were still active members but this was uncommon. Since it was more likely that the terrorists left the organisation to hide out in countries like Latin America and France for long periods of time to avoid being arrested.

Finally, the vast majority of former members decided to quit, often during a very long prison sentence. Or because of the development of new reasons, like becoming a father.

On the whole, I wanted to show you that the research suggests that there is absolutely no one reason explaining why terrorists quit organisations, because there is a lot of internal and external reasons explaining why this happens.

Yet there were patterns and it seems clear that people flat out didn't abandon their terrorist ideology and radicalisation because of guilt. That is almost the only reason we can rule out for why people quit terror organisations.

Moreover, building upon the patterns in the ending of terrorist organisations, Miller (2012) studied the statistical patterns of the onset and decline of terrorist organisations using data from the global terrorism database. This database contains data on over 500 groups active between 1970 and 2008. As well as for the terror groups to be included in the study they had to have been active for at least a year.

Miller found there were two major patterns, which were 80% of terrorist groups had a rapid decline from terrorism activity after their peak year of attack, whereas only 20% had a minimal decline after peak year.

In other words, it was the terrorist organisations that had fast-climbing onset curves for attacks that were the most likely to achieve moderate to high levels of attacks per year. As well as terrorist organisations can show rapid or steady decline after their peak year. So the majority of terror groups fall quickly after their peak year but some groups survive a little longer and manage a slow decline in activity.

Although, as I mentioned earlier and I doubt there is much empirical research on the topic given how new this topic is in the literature, but it's critical to understand that just because one terror group ends. It still may signal the start of a new terrorist organisation, like a splinter terror group. For example, how the New IRA rose from the ashes of the original IRA.

So after being introduced to the forensic psychology of terrorism, what's the research behind hostage taking?

I'm really looking forward to the next section because the research improves and we talk about some utterly fascinating findings. So turn over the page and let's learn about hostage situations.

INTRODUCTION TO HOSTAGE BARRICADE INCIDENTS

Moving onto the last section of the book, I am very excited to look at Hostage Barricade Incidents, which I have to admit is a very technical name for hostage situations. And I'm interested in these types of crimes because they are a great plot device in a lot of TV, movies and books as well as I have been known to use a hostage situation from time to time. For example, in my enthralling, gripping private eye novella *Cops, Robbers and Private Eyes*.

However, let's see how these Hostage Barricade Incidents work in reality and how can we use forensic psychology research to better understand these complex, deadly and distressing situations.

As a result, you can probably imagine, Hostage Barricade Incidents describes when the police and security services besiege a place where people are being held against their will. Also, these situations differ from a "normal" or "simple" siege because these sieges don't involve hostages. In these situations the police are trying to get a person out of a physical location.

Whereas in Hostage Barricade Incidents, it isn't the police that are more likely to determine what action is taken and when like in a siege, instead it is the hostage takers that are more likely to determine the action taken by everyone.

One example of this is that the police cannot simply storm in and try to forcibly release the hostages because this is extremely risky and the hostage takers are probably prepared for this action. And you only need to go online to see the different cases when the police had tried to force the release of hostages and hostages have been killed as a result.

Consequently, in Hostage Barricade Incidents, it is flat out critical that there is some form of assessment that takes place so the police and other professionals can be aware of the risk of a forceful intervention compared to continuing the barricade into the future.

This is important to understand for information I'll share later in the book.

To test this in the real-world, Yokota, Iwami, Watanabe, Fiyita and Watanabe (2004) studied risk factors that they established from real-life hostage incidents and compared them to the beliefs police officers have about different aspects of the incidents.

The results show that in real-life Hostage

Barricade Incidents, 50% of them had firearms present. So this was a rather poor indicator of risk because firearm use is very common in Hostage Barricade Incidents.

In addition, the researchers found that hostages were more likely to be injured when they were in a domestic setting and when domestic violence was a motive, or when the purpose of the hostage situation was to get ex-partner back with them.

Personally, I always have find that reason very interesting because in my mind, it just doesn't compute because I don't understand how taking a lot of people hostage is going to make anyone fall in love and want to be with someone. And even if that did work, I think for someone to find that attractive and want to get with someone, then my question is, what the hell is wrong with them and if that's what they find attractive then you probably don't want to be with them.

Anyway, that's just my two cents.

Furthermore, the researchers found that expressive situations like suicide, suicide attempts and domestic violence were all more likely to lead to injury. As well as what I find interesting is that the risk of hostages being injured was actually rather low if the perpetrator had a mental health condition.

In addition, the researchers found that 73% of Japanese Police Officers believed if they were in a highly excited state, this was dangerous for hostage takers. In reality, if we look at real-life incidents, it is the longer sieges that increase the risk of death.

Despite the overall risk of hostage deaths being small because fewer than 4% of Hostage Barricade Incidents result in deaths.

The second most common perceived risk factor was "an accident is caused due to interpersonal problems" because this was mentioned by 24% of police officers and the other risk factors are listed below:

- 16% of police officers said telling hostages their demands couldn't be met was risky.

- 33% of officers mentioned offence characteristics were risky. These offence characteristics include a hostage taker's mental health and if they had ever attempted suicide, and drug use.

- 16% of officers mentioned the police were risk factors. For example, if no effective communication between the police and hostage takers could be established.

The second part of Yokota, Iwami, Watanabe, Fiyita and Watanabe (2004) involved getting the police officers to look at 22 possible Hostage Barricade Incidents and getting them to evaluate the risk involved in each one. The descriptions in each of these scenarios included if the hostages were killed or injured, how long the siege was in duration and if the hostage taker had demanded an escape route. As well as there if there was a plane hijacked and if the hostage takers had done this as part of some political action or group. For example, a right-wing terrorism group.

The results showed that generally all these details and risk factors were rated as high risk. When hostages had been injured this was deemed the most high risk, followed by the hostage takers taking illegal drugs followed by the takers being mentally "ill" (I hate that term but it is what is sadly used in the literature).

In addition, the results showed that the police officers rated some low-risk characteristics too. For example, a hostage situation was deemed low risk when the hostage takers made reasonable demands to the police, like demands for money, and when the hostage situation was covered by the media as was the means of escape.

Furthermore, this I don't find very surprising but it is always good to have beliefs confirmed by research. The study found that the police rated emotional and impulsive situations as riskier than instrumental ones. In other words, the police officers believed it is more dangerous and risky when someone has taken hostages because they're extremely emotional, desperate and they haven't put much thought or planning in this.

However, if you've read my book *Police Psychology* then you'll probably be familiar with how there is a difference (sometimes a massive difference) between the beliefs of police officers and what the research says actually happens. These hostage incidents are no different. Due to the researchers found there was a very weak relationship between what police officers judged as risky situations and the injuries and deaths that occurred.

As a result, one obvious conclusion from the study is that officers were unaware of the nature of risk in these hostage situations. Now, this could be a result of inexperience but the study's sample were the sort of officers who would be in control of early stages of hostage negotiations as well as the barricade, so these are the exact sort of people that need to have good awareness of risk early on.

A piece of evidence possibly supporting the argument that this conclusion is a result of inexperience is that 80% of police officers involved in major incidents have less than 5 years of policing experience.

Building upon this further, this idea of a lack of experience can be showed in a model used for senior UK officers who manage major incidents as described by Crego and Alison (2004). Since police officers perceived themselves as having a lack of control and they believe they're going to get the blame whatever happens here as would their managers, so this doesn't help the situation. This results in the police officers deeming hostage situations as complex and difficult to deal with, this is only increased by feelings of lack of experience.

To further research this, Crego and Alison (2004) used electronic conferencing to bring together a range of officers who had managed major incidents in the past. Then they all systematically explored the experience of each person and how they managed the incident.

The aspects of the situation the study looked at included an unstructured account from each person so they told everyone about their experiences and outlined significant issue with the incidents. Then they were given a building, split into teams and they all reviewed the data from the first stage to build on it and there was a plenary session were themes were developed and agreed by everyone.

The results of this study found that professionals focused on prioritisation during hostage incidents because the participants rated different issues according to different criteria. For example, in order of implementation and the impact it would have on the situation. As well as officers used two co-occurring issues as defining features of criticality of incident.

In addition, two important features named by the participants as having a direct impact on hostage barricade incidents are creating a good team atmosphere and keeping both local as well as national police agencies informed.

Then whether the issue would affect how other people judged the police impacted their response. For example, how victims, the local community and media would judge them. This is why police officers try to engage with the media early on in a situation, they anticipate leaks and they appreciate the media as a source of information for them.

Therefore, now we've been introduced to hostage situations, let's see how hostage negotiations work and why they're so important in these potentially deadly situations.

HOSTAGE NEGOTIATIONS

One of my favourite TV series of all time has to be the brilliant programme called "Ransom" which follows a hostage negotiator as he and his team travel the world trying to resolve hostage situations peacefully and they tend to solve larger crimes along the way. Of course, I know full-well that this programme doesn't reflect real hostage situations perfectly and there are probably a few artistic liberties the writers took, but it feels real. And it definitely got me interested in our current chapter.

As a result, the reason why hostage-taking is a separate section of the book is because whilst hostage taking is a terrorist technique, it is more likely to occur in domestic crimes. Such as, armed robberies. And because these crimes are complex and potentially deadly, the practicalities of how to deal with these situations has been addressed by a lot of people, including psychologists.

Part of the reason why psychologists are

interested in hostage-taking is because these extreme situations might have a core of morality and there are a lot of psychological factors and processes happening here. Even more so when we consider the hostage takers- police relationship that occurs in these incidents.

This led to Wilson and Smith (2010) proposing that behaviours in hostage takings are bound by 2 rules sets. Firstly, rules about the "normal" behaviour that should be glowed in these situations (in other words what the hostage takers believe is normal in a hostage situation) and these hostage-taking behaviours are bound by rules about everyday behaviour that act as fallbacks if the specific rules cannot be applied.

Furthermore, Wilson and Smith (2010) propose the following are important to understand in these situations. The motivation for the incident is important and this might be complex to figure out but clues to these motivations could be in the behaviour showed in the situation. Since according to Wilson and Smith if the hostage takers only demand money then the incident is personally motivated, not politically.

Whereas if the demand is for the release of fellow terrorists then the hostage takers could be attempting to fill a gap in the organisation. As well as a demand to release prisoners more generally could simply be about terrorist ideology about the perceived injustice of it all.

Another aspect that is important to understand is the level of planning and resources, because the amount of planning could tell us various things. For example, it could indicate the terrorist's determination to fulfil their mission. Also, the terrorist's behaviour should be predictable compared to random incidents. And in case you're wondering how the police would know the level of planning, one such indicator would be the amount of resources the hostage takers have.

What Are The Rules For Negotiation?

As we continue our look at Wilson and Smith (2010), the researchers suggested a number of rules that negotiators should use in crisis negotiations. For example, Wilson and Smith (2010) strongly believed both parties (the police and the hostage takers) should show that they are willing to negotiate, as well as both parties can show this willingness by several different actions. Such as being willing to extent deadlines to the other party.

Another rule is that the hostages are the currency of this exchange so the terrorists or hostage takes might bargain and/ or negotiate with them. Yet if the hostage takers release all the hostages then this is a bad strategy as only the building or aircraft or whatever the hostage takers are in remain to be bargained with.

On the other hand, if the hostage takers do not release some of the hostages then this is a bad strategy as well. Since this shows they are unwilling to negotiate and this violates the first rule of negotiation. Also, there are other reasons why hostage takers should release some of the hostages because this can earn them good publicity and even more so if some of the released people are women, children and the sick.

On the whole, Wilson and Smith (2010) suggest that deviating from these rules of negotiation might lead to a direct response from the authorities. They give examples about the terrorists bluffing, for instance, about number or whether they have hostages in the first place, because negotiations tend to break down here if this happens.

Guidelines For Hostage Negotiation

Another study that helps to shred some light on how hostage negotiations work in the real world is Flood (2003) who found that 82% of hostage incidents are dealt with without any death or injuries to hostages or hostage takers. This is probably mainly a result of the modern crisis negotiation techniques introduced by Frank Bolz and Harvey Schlossberg of the New York Police Department in the early 1970s.

Now this is interesting because Schlossberg had a doctorate in clinical psychology (Strentz, 2006), and that's only really interesting to me because that's my background, but it means he was very psychologically and academically minded.

The two researchers worked together after the Munich Olympics Massacre where the police tactic used had been disastrous, so the researchers wanted to produce solid guidelines for negotiators in these situations.

Therefore, instead of the hard-nosed, confrontational tactics of the past, Frank Bolz and Harvey Schlossberg introduced new techniques based on conflict and dispute resolution.

Overall, the fundamental principle of their new approach was to buy more time for the police to find a rational ending to the incident, and this approach is critical because it is the fundamental approach that modern negotiations are based on.

In addition, some other parts of the guidelines include how any negotiation with hostage takers takes place whilst the police are focused on containing them in their environment at the same time as they're trying to meet the demands of the takers.

Also, Frank Bolz and Harvey Schlossberg suggest police officers should use whatever methods are available to them to understand the motives of the hostage takers and personality factors that might underline the incident.

With an extremely important aspect being that the police officers to proceed with the negotiations at a purposefully slow pace to stretch out the time for negotiating. This is a possible way of dealing with the already stretched emotion of the hostage takers by giving them more time to express how they feel and so on might react in a more rational way.

The Sheer Importance Of Active Listening Skills In

Hostage Negotiations

To wrap up this chapter on hostage negotiations before we move onto the various models, we need to talk about "Active listening skills" because this is a phrase used to describe strategies like mirroring and emotional labelling that is involving in the formation of a relationship between the hostage takers and the negotiators. Hopefully, leading to a diffusion of the situation.

Noesner and Webster (1997) describes different types of active listening skills used in these types of the situation. For example, paraphrasing, this is where the hostage takers' words are repeated back by the negotiator in their own words to show the hostage takers they're being listened too. Also, open ended questions are a good example because these are the only way to learn what's going on. Since when the hostage takers do most of the talking, it means they're giving longer responses and they can reveal more information to the negotiators.

In addition, another example of active listening is minimal encouragement. This is where the negotiators show the hostage takers they're listening by keeping the conversation going and this can result in control of the situation shifting to the negotiator. Everyday examples of these "encouragements" include "okay" and "I see".

Also, you can have emotional labelling where the negotiator needs to deal with the hostage taker's emotion about the incident. So the negotiator gives the hostage taker's emotion a tentative label. For example, "you seen to be angry with how the English have treated Muslims in their country," then the taker's response to the statement allows the negotiator to learn more.

Furthermore, mirroring involves repeating a few words of what the hostage taker just said. Such as if the taker said "I won't let some English push me around," the negotiator might say "You won't let the English push you around,". This is effective because it avoids a confrontational stance between the takers and the police and it might reveal more information.

Finally, "I" messages can be useful because these are non-confrontational personal comments that the negotiator makes in response in the hostage taker's words actions. For example, them talking about their own frustration about lack of professional negotiators.

Thankfully, a person doesn't have to be a born negotiator to be good at it, because hostage negotiation can be a taught skill in police training programmes.

Due to Perera et al. (2006) evaluated a training programme with psychological, suicide prevention, basic negotiation principles and more taught through role play. Then FBI agents took part in the role play assessment before and after the intensive training. As well as the role-play for the negotiation skills were based on real-life audio tapes from incidents.

The results showed that the agents' active listening generally improved after the training.

Nonetheless, one interesting finding from the study was that problem solving decreased after training. And it is suggested that this might be a good thing because it is dangerous if the police officers try to come on with a solution before any rapport has been developed between the police and the hostage takers. Therefore, if problem solving happens in the early stages of incidents then this could very well increase the likelihood of a pre-emptive intervention so this is dangerous for everyone involved.

On the whole, it's clear that hostage negotiation skills can be taught, but there is evidence that these active listening skills aren't used in practice.

This mainly comes from Webster (2004) who listened to audiotapes from real life incidents and the study found that only 13% used active listening skills. And out of 13%, 66% of these skills were minor encouragements. Such as very basic acknowledgements that the negotiators was listening. Like repeating what was said.

Also, complex active listening skills were a much smaller total of the 13%. For example, 66% might have been minor encouragement but 12% was paraphrasing, 8% of total was emotional labelling, 7% of total was summarising and 6% of the officer's turn to speak was mirroring. If minor encouragements were taken out only 6% of the total are active listening skills. That's a decrease of 7%.

Overall, whilst research shows that active listening skills are flat out critical in real-world hostage negotiations, it is a shame and clear that these skills are not being used in practice.

So now we've been introduced to hostage negotiations and the different skills and concepts and rules needed for them, I wonder are there any psychological models that bring all this knowledge together?

MODELS OF HOSTAGE NEGOTIATION

As most of the readers of this book are going to be university psychology students or psychology professionals, I think it is safe to say that we are all aware of psychology's love of models. Us psychologists flat out love a good model to help explain stuff, how different processes work and models seem to be the cool thing to do in psychology.

Of course, I am well aware that psychological models are really important and they are very useful in helping us conceptualise and understand different psychological processes.

However, when it comes to hostage negotiations these models can be a little… silly to some extent. Since there are so many different models and most of them are just theoretical with only a handful of them actually being evidence-based.

Some reason or piece of supporting evidence for why the empirical research literature on terrorism is so dire and just awful.

Then again, I need to remind all of us, including myself, that most of the time psychologists do adopt the empirical models but as we know from previous chapters, conducting empirical work on terrorism is very difficult or next to impossible.

Overall, the entire purpose of a psychological model is to offer researchers a way to clarify a very difficult and complex problem into something that is easier to understand. Of course, there are massive problems with this approach because we are probably trying to "dumb down" massive psychological concepts into a nice, tidy little model. Yet that argument is outside the scope of this book.

In addition, this lack of evidence-based models needs to be addressed urgently because crisis negotiations are deadly issues were people could die if a mistake is made, so it is critical that we understand how these negotiations work. Both in a theoretical sense and in a real-world sense.

In addition, different models provide police officers with a shared framework and a basis for going forward with any crisis negotiations. With the wonderfully added caveat (that protects the authors of models from blame) that all models need to be used flexibly and police officers might need to move back a stage as the negotiations go forward.

FBI's Behavioural Influence Stairway Model of Crisis Negotiation

This model of crisis negotiation was created by Vecchi, Van Hasselt and Romano (2005) and according to Ireland and Vecchi (2009), this was a protype version of this sort of model that went onto influenced strategies in UK.

Therefore, FBI's Behavioural Influence Stairway Model of Crisis Negotiation is the updated version of the original FBI model. As well as the stairway metaphor is common in crisis negotiation models, because the stairway starts at the bottom where there is no relationship between the negotiators and hostage takers. Then it ends at the top of the stairs where there is a good relationship between the hostage takers and negotiators.

When it comes to how the negotiators get from the bottom step to the top step, the progress is done by active listening skills over time and a few other factors that we'll look at in this chapter. Yet these steps are flexible to circumstances because sometimes negotiators just don't have time to build a relationship like they normally would.

Moreover, there is no reason for negotiators to take a step down in face of difficulty. As well as there's no fixed time scale, negotiators don't need to know anything about if the hostage takers have any mental health conditions and negotiators don't really need to know their motives for this model.

Section:
What Is The Process Of Bringing The Incident To Peaceful Resolution?

We all probably know by now that the underlying

aim of hostage negotiation is to build a relationship between the police and the hostage takers by developing trust and positive relationships. The aim of hostage negotiations are not to understand the motives of the hostage taker.

The reason for this is because if you concentrate on the motives then this causes a divergence away from the emotionally driven aspects of the situation and can make matters worse.

Also, it's important to note that hostage negotiators are not there to solve the problems of the terrorists.

I'm mentioning all of this because building a relationship in "normal" circumstances requires a lot of give and take, a lot of time and a lot of effort from both parties. You don't have this time and other luxuries in a hostage situation, so there is a stairway dynamic and terrorists might alternate between different steps of these models.

Then if we cast our minds back to the last chapter, active listening skills can be critical and they can thought of as moving a terrorist from a place of emotionally to rationality, so you can talk them down and end the situation peacefully.

As a result, the stages used in this FBI model are empathy, rapport and influence. Yet thankfully, there is a lot of flexibility in the model and this is important because as I just mentioned, relationships go back and forth on the steps. But the model is still useful as it brings a sense of structure to a situation that is often chaotic to the negotiator involved.

Moreover, Madrignal, Bowman and McClain (2009) suggested a 4 phase model that focuses on the action of the negotiator and indicates what style of negotiation to take. These phases are establishing the initial dialogue, building rapport, influencing and surrender. As well as all these phases require different types of verbal statements so they change throughout the process and backtracking is possible to. Also, it's important that this process isn't done too quickly as this could result in the hostage takers becoming angry or have some sort of other reaction.

And talking more generally for a moment, phase 1 needs to be done correctly to stop the taker's response becoming very negative in phase 2. Hence, why active listening skills are critical.

When it comes to establishing the initial dialogue, the police are assuming that the hostage taker could be reluctant to talk to a negotiator and maybe hostile. So this stage is about creating a dialogue by whatever means are appropriate. Once a dialogue is created, the initial statements used by the negotiators are more general and about the situation compared to later stages. Some topics can actually include the weather and talking about the condition of the hostages and even a sports game if the hostage situation is happening on a day of a big match. Although, this phase is difficult because the hostage taker might not want to talk to the police or any negotiator.

In terms of building rapport, the purpose of this stage is to create a personal relationship between the hostage taker and the negotiator where the free exchange of personal information becomes available.

Also, a negotiator can know if they've been successful in this stage because the hostage taker will be able to tell them information including things about their emotions.

Penultimately, there is the influencing with the task of this stage meaning the negotiator needs to persuade the hostage takers to free the hostages and bring the stand-off to a peaceful end. The risk at this stage is if the hostage taker believes the negotiator is trying to trick them into something then this can get risky very quickly. Thankfully, because there is already a personal relationship between the taker and the negotiator, there aren't many active listening skills needed here so the negotiator might be able to make suggestions, promises and try to reframe the situation as a positive outcome for surrender.

And even the negotiator providing solutions to the problem and bargaining could be a part of this phase, this isn't the focus. The focus will always be communicating to the hostage taker about the safety of surrender peacefully.

Finally, surrender is obviously when the hostage taker has decided to surrender. Then it becomes the job of the negotiator to give the hostage takers instructions about how to do it safely and ensure takers know what is required.

I do personally quite like this model because it seems good, useful and rather practical which in these sort of situations is always good.

On the whole, the model might not be built on vast amounts of research but it is extremely useful in conceptualising and breaking down the negotiation process so negotiators can structure their experiences around a meaningful framework.

Therefore, in this book, so far we've looked at terrorism and hostage taking as two rather separate things, what happens when we combine them? What does the research say about terrorists that take hostages?

HOW TERRORISM LINKS TO HOSTAGE-TAKING?

For the final chapter of the book, we are going to be bringing everything together, because I suppose some of you might have been wondering why we were looking at terrorism and hostage taking situations as very different things. The reason for that is because generally speaking, they are really easy to treat as separate things but sometimes hostage takings are linked to terrorism.

As a result, whilst most hostage takings aren't linked to terrorism, this does happen but this is problematic for the research literature because it strains our current research. Which to be honest by this point in the book, I think it is fair to say that it doesn't exactly take much to strain our current research. And yes I know I don't have a very high opinion of this current literature but considering how artificial and how unempirical it is, I don't really think you can blame me.

Anyway, a brilliant research example but a
terrible event in human history of when an act of
terrorism involves a hostage situation is the Belsan
school attack that left over 300 adults and children
dead in 2004. This incident involved 1200 hostages
with many of them being children and they were
taken by 50 strategically placed hostage takers.

This was made even worse by the fact that 21
people were killed on the first day of the attack and
the bodies were thrown out of windows for everyone
outside to see.

Also, the terrorists were very clever because they
not only had 4 terrorists in a single area, but any 1 of
these 4 terrorists in that single area could explode all
130 explosives in other parts of the school.

In addition, the terrorists made impossible
demands and this is where you know they were well-
prepared. The terrorists made use of gasmasks so that
eliminated a wide range of options for the police, and
there were angry parents outside the school
threatening to kill the rescuers if they didn't try to
intervene.

As you can imagine the situation was always only
going to have one single outcome. There would be a
lot of deaths and I think this is a fascinating example
because this was a very well thoughtful terror attack,
and if one of my books ever needed an extremely
thoughtful hostage situation, I would probably draw
on this awful incident for inspiration.

As a result of this incident and others, Dolnick and Fitzgerald (2011) painted a picture of "new terrorists" and this is for a few reasons. Yet new terrorists are difficult to read because they typically study and read hostage taking incident reports and they read hostage crisis training manuals. As well as this new breed of terrorists seem more willing to harm hostages to achieve their aims.

In addition, this new breed seems to have good tactical knowledge so it's difficult to use threats coercively and to bargain hard, because these groups have good weapons and they are prepared to die. As well as they have good communication with fellow terrorists at different locations, and this links back to what I spoke about at the beginning of the book about new waves of terrorism follow advancements in technology.

A final reason or concern surrounding this new breed of terrorists comes from their use of religious rhetoric because there has always been religious rhetoric in terrorism, but the rhetoric used by this new breed of terrorist is extreme and goes far beyond what negotiators have experienced in general.

Therefore, there needs to be resources available to help negotiations as suggested by Dolnick and Fitzgerald.

Since negotiations are about influencing the thinking, decision-making and the behaviour of another person, and just talking with a terrorist or hostage taker can help to provide the negotiators with important information.

When it comes to dealing with terrorists, negotiators need to remember that they're negotiating with a rational person, regardless of the extremeness of their actions. And this I think is always important to bear in mind, in everyday life (let alone dealing with terrorists) there are countless examples of actions we don't personally understand but these actions are perfectly logical to that individual. For example, if we quickly think about depression, to you and me, it makes no sense not doing activities we enjoy to improve our mood, but to a depressed person it is perfectly logical not to do that because they are simply too hard to do and they'll fail at it and all the other negative cognitive processes.

My point is if negotiators start thinking of them as terrorists then this can conjure up stereotypes of terrorism and this might very well be counterproductive. Especially, when we consider that in mainstream society, terrorists are thought to be dumb, irrational, crazy zealots that wouldn't know sense if it bit them in the private area. The reality is very different, something I hope I've showed you in this book.

Therefore, negotiators need to constantly question their assumptions, biases and their characteristics of the terrorists to make sure that they aren't falling into its biased cognitive processes. For example, if the negotiators jump to conclusions then this could result in them missing opportunities for more information that is correct compared to the assumptions the negotiators are making up as well.

Another guideline for negotiation is negotiators should look for a way to empathically address any grievances underlying the hostage taking and terrorist action, because this can make it more difficult for the terrorists to label the authorities negatively as being unreasonable.

In addition, active listening skills should always be used to get as full a picture as possible about terrorist's motives and grievances, so asking in detail for a justification of the action could be good here.

Overall, there isn't a great amount of research when it comes to terrorism and hostage-taking, let alone when you combine the two areas. Therefore, whilst this is an extremely important research area, it is advancing very slowly on a rather insecurely based that absolutely has to be improved over time.

CONCLUSION

I have to admit that I have really enjoyed this book because it's fun to look at terrorism and hostage-taking from a forensic psychology viewpoint. Since forensic psychology allows us to explore criminal behaviour in an empirical manner and it allows us to overcome the myths and misconceptions that society creates to help itself understand awful actions. This is what we saw in the second chapter when we found that despite popular belief, terrorism is not caused by personality factors or mental health conditions.

In addition, I really enjoyed learning about what actually makes a terrorist, because we might not have all the answers. In fact, we certainly do not have most of the answers, but we are slowly starting to understand stuff and we have finally recognised that it is a wide range of factors that start and maintain someone going on the long road to becoming a terrorist.

Personally, I actually believe this is a good thing. I think it's good that it's a long road and it is a process. It means that there is time, there are opportunities and there is hope of "saving" that person before they become an active terrorist that attacks and kills people.

That is why looking at terrorism and hostage-taking is so important because it is all about hope. Giving us a sense of hope that we can understand this awful behaviour and we can create interventions and support the people that are more likely to become terrorists.

Of course, there are massive research problems and I will never excuse some of the poor research practices. I get researching terrorism is an impossible task but at least these researchers are trying. They might not always succeed and they certainly need to improve their practices to improve their research, but I do appreciate them trying.

All research areas have to start somewhere and I think if we look at all research areas in all sciences, there were questionable things going on in the early days for all of them. But research into terrorism must improve if it is ever going to have the power that it needs, if this research is ever going to have a meaningful impact in society against terrorism.

Therefore, I truly hope that you've learnt a lot from this book and that you're enjoyed it. I know that I have and I look forward to exploring forensic psychology even more in the coming years because forensic psychology is a lot of fun.

Because who doesn't love exploring the darker side of human behaviour. I know I do and I'm willing to say if you're made it to the end of this book, then you probably do to.

REFERENCES

Abbasi, I., Khatwani, M. K., & Soomro, H. A. (2018). A review of psycho-social theories of terrorism. *Grassroots*, *51*(2).

Borum, R. (2004). Psychology of terrorism.

Braithwaite, A. (2013). The logic of public fear in terrorism and counter-terrorism. *Journal of police and criminal psychology*, *28*, 95-101.

DiMaggio, C., & Galea, S. (2006). The behavioral consequences of terrorism: a meta-analysis. *Academic emergency medicine*, *13*(5), 559-566.

DiMaggio, C., Galea, S., & Richardson, L. D. (2007). Emergency department visits for behavioral and mental health care after a terrorist attack. *Annals of Emergency Medicine*, *50*(3), 327-334.

Ferguson, N., & Kamble, S. V. (2012). The role of revenge, denial, and terrorism distress in restoring just world beliefs: the impact of the 2008 Mumbai attacks on British and Indian students. *The Journal of social psychology*, *152*(6), 687-696.

Foster, D. M., Braithwaite, A., & Sobek, D. (2013). There can be no compromise: Institutional inclusiveness, fractionalization and domestic terrorism. *British Journal of Political Science*, *43*(3), 541-557.

Fujita, G., Watanabe, K., Yokota, K., Kuraishi, H., Suzuki, M., Wachi, T., & Otsuka, Y. (2013). Multivariate models for behavioral offender profiling of Japanese homicide. *Criminal Justice and Behavior*, *40*(2), 214-227.

Gabriel, R., Ferrando, L., Cortón, E. S., Mingote, C., García-Camba, E., Liria, A. F., & Galea, S. (2007). Psychopathological consequences after a terrorist attack: An epidemiological study among victims, the general population, and police officers☆. *European Psychiatry*, *22*(6), 339-346.

Howitt, D. (2015). *Introduction to forensic and criminal psychology*. Pearson Education.

Hudson, R. A. (2007). The sociology and psychology of terrorism: Who becomes a terrorist and why?.

Jhangiani, R. (2010). Psychological concomitants of the 11 September 2001 terrorist attacks: A review. *Behavioral Sciences of Terrorism and Political Aggression*, *2*(1), 38-69.

Lipkus, I. (1991). The construction and preliminary validation of a global belief in a just world scale and the exploratory analysis of the multidimensional belief in a just world scale. *Personality and Individual differences*, *12*(11), 1171-1178.

Lomborg, B., & Sandler, T. (2008). Re-thinking

counter-terrorism. *Daily News Egypt*.

Mythen, G., & Walklate, S. (2006). Criminology and terrorism: Which thesis? Risk society or governmentality?. *British journal of criminology*, *46*(3), 379-398.

Post, J. M., McGinnis, C., & Moody, K. (2014). The changing face of terrorism in the 21st century: The communications revolution and the virtual community of hatred. *Behavioral sciences & the law*, *32*(3), 306-334.

Silker, E. S. (2004). Terrorists, interrogation, and torture: Where do we draw the line. *J. Legis.*, *31*, 191.

Yokota, K., Fujita, G., Watanabe, K., Yoshimoto, K., & Wachi, T. (2007). Application of the behavioral investigative support system for profiling perpetrators of serial sexual assaults. *Behavioral Sciences & the Law*, *25*(6), 841-856.

GET YOUR EXCLUSIVE FREE 8 BOOK PSYCHOLOGY BOXSET AND YOUR EMAIL PSYCHOLOGY COURSE HERE!

https://www.subscribepage.io/psychologybo
xset

CHECK OUT THE PSYCHOLOGY WORLD PODCAST FOR MORE PSYCHOLOGY INFORMATION! AVAILABLE ON ALL MAJOR PODCAST APPS.

About the author:

Connor Whiteley is the author of over 60 books in the sci-fi fantasy, nonfiction psychology and books for writer's genre and he is a Human Branding Speaker and Consultant.

He is a passionate warhammer 40,000 reader, psychology student and author.

Who narrates his own audiobooks and he hosts The Psychology World Podcast.

All whilst studying Psychology at the University of Kent, England.

Also, he was a former Explorer Scout where he gave a speech to the Maltese President in August 2018 and he attended Prince Charles' 70th Birthday Party at Buckingham Palace in May 2018.

Plus, he is a self-confessed coffee lover!

All books in 'An Introductory Series':
Clinical Psychology and Transgender Clients
Clinical Psychology
Careers In Psychology
Psychology of Suicide
Dementia Psychology
Clinical Psychology Reflections Volume 4
Forensic Psychology of Terrorism And Hostage-Taking
Forensic Psychology of False Allegations
Year In Psychology
CBT For Anxiety
CBT For Depression
Applied Psychology
BIOLOGICAL PSYCHOLOGY 3RD EDITION
COGNITIVE PSYCHOLOGY THIRD EDITION
SOCIAL PSYCHOLOGY- 3RD EDITION
ABNORMAL PSYCHOLOGY 3RD EDITION
PSYCHOLOGY OF RELATIONSHIPS- 3RD EDITION
DEVELOPMENTAL PSYCHOLOGY 3RD EDITION
HEALTH PSYCHOLOGY
RESEARCH IN PSYCHOLOGY

A GUIDE TO MENTAL HEALTH AND
TREATMENT AROUND THE WORLD-
A GLOBAL LOOK AT DEPRESSION
FORENSIC PSYCHOLOGY
THE FORENSIC PSYCHOLOGY OF
THEFT, BURGLARY AND OTHER
CRIMES AGAINST PROPERTY
CRIMINAL PROFILING: A FORENSIC
PSYCHOLOGY GUIDE TO FBI
PROFILING AND GEOGRAPHICAL
AND STATISTICAL PROFILING.
CLINICAL PSYCHOLOGY
FORMULATION IN PSYCHOTHERAPY
PERSONALITY PSYCHOLOGY AND
INDIVIDUAL DIFFERENCES
CLINICAL PSYCHOLOGY
REFLECTIONS VOLUME 1
CLINICAL PSYCHOLOGY
REFLECTIONS VOLUME 2
Clinical Psychology Reflections Volume 3
CULT PSYCHOLOGY
Police Psychology

A Psychology Student's Guide To University
How Does University Work?
A Student's Guide To University And
Learning

University Mental Health and Mindset

Other books by Connor Whiteley:
Bettie English Private Eye Series
A Very Private Woman
The Russian Case
A Very Urgent Matter
A Case Most Personal
Trains, Scots and Private Eyes
The Federation Protects
Cops, Robbers and Private Eyes
Just Ask Bettie English
An Inheritance To Die For
The Death of Graham Adams
Bearing Witness
The Twelve
The Wrong Body
The Assassination Of Bettie English
Wining And Dying
Eight Hours
Uniformed Cabal
A Case Most Christmas

Gay Romance Novellas
Breaking, Nursing, Repairing A Broken Heart
Jacob And Daniel
Fallen For A Lie
Spying And Weddings

Clean Break
Awakening Love
Meeting A Country Man
Loving Prime Minister
Snowed In Love
Never Been Kissed
Love Betrays You

Lord of War Origin Trilogy:
Not Scared Of The Dark
Madness
Burn Them All

The Fireheart Fantasy Series
Heart of Fire
Heart of Lies
Heart of Prophecy
Heart of Bones
Heart of Fate

City of Assassins (Urban Fantasy)
City of Death
City of Martyrs
City of Pleasure
City of Power

Agents of The Emperor
Return of The Ancient Ones
Vigilance
Angels of Fire
Kingmaker
The Eight
The Lost Generation
Hunt
Emperor's Council
Speaker of Treachery
Birth Of The Empire
Terraforma
Spaceguard

The Rising Augusta Fantasy Adventure Series
Rise To Power
Rising Walls
Rising Force
Rising Realm

Lord Of War Trilogy (Agents of The Emperor)
Not Scared Of The Dark
Madness
Burn It All Down

Miscellaneous:
RETURN
FREEDOM
SALVATION
Reflection of Mount Flame
The Masked One
The Great Deer
English Independence

OTHER SHORT STORIES BY CONNOR WHITELEY

Mystery Short Story Collections
Criminally Good Stories Volume 1: 20
Detective Mystery Short Stories
Criminally Good Stories Volume 2: 20 Private
Investigator Short Stories
Criminally Good Stories Volume 3: 20 Crime
Fiction Short Stories
Criminally Good Stories Volume 4: 20
Science Fiction and Fantasy Mystery Short
Stories
Criminally Good Stories Volume 5: 20
Romantic Suspense Short Stories

Mystery Short Stories:
Protecting The Woman She Hated
Finding A Royal Friend

Our Woman In Paris
Corrupt Driving
A Prime Assassination
Jubilee Thief
Jubilee, Terror, Celebrations
Negative Jubilation
Ghostly Jubilation
Killing For Womenkind
A Snowy Death
Miracle Of Death
A Spy In Rome
The 12:30 To St Pancreas
A Country In Trouble
A Smokey Way To Go
A Spicy Way To GO
A Marketing Way To Go
A Missing Way To Go
A Showering Way To Go
Poison In The Candy Cane
Kendra Detective Mystery Collection Volume 1
Kendra Detective Mystery Collection Volume 2
Mystery Short Story Collection Volume 1
Mystery Short Story Collection Volume 2
Criminal Performance
Candy Detectives

Key To Birth In The Past

Science Fiction Short Stories:
Their Brave New World
Gummy Bear Detective
The Candy Detective
What Candies Fear
The Blurred Image
Shattered Legions
The First Rememberer
Life of A Rememberer
System of Wonder
Lifesaver
Remarkable Way She Died
The Interrogation of Annabella Stormic
Blade of The Emperor
Arbiter's Truth
Computation of Battle
Old One's Wrath
Puppets and Masters
Ship of Plague
Interrogation
Edge of Failure

Fantasy Short Stories:
City of Snow
City of Light

City of Vengeance
Dragons, Goats and Kingdom
Smog The Pathetic Dragon
Don't Go In The Shed
The Tomato Saver
The Remarkable Way She Died
Dragon Coins
Dragon Tea
Dragon Rider

9 781917 181730